To My Girls

A Look at Friendship from the Perspective of 8 Women

By Visionary Author Shannon Wilkerson

Contributing Authors: Toni Wilkerson, Farrah McBride, Ilka Tamar, LaToya Mack, Bonnetta Petties- Simmons, Megan Johnson, Tylisha Cutler-Hagood

Scripture quotations marked KJV are taken from the King James Version of the bible.

Scripture quotations marked NLT are taken from the HOLY BIBLE, NEW LIVING TRANSLATION, Copyright© 1996, 2004, 2007 by Tyndale House Foundation. Used by permission of Tyndale House Publishers, Inc., Carol Stream, Illinois 60188. All rights reserved. Used by permission.

TO MY GIRLS. Copyright 2020 by Shannon Wilkerson

All rights reserved. No part of this book may be reproduced or transmitted in any form or by any means, electronic or mechanical, including photocopying and recording, or by information storage and retrieval, without permission in writing from author and publisher.

Please direct all copyright inquiries to: shanni@shanniwilke.com

Printed in the United States of America
FIRST EDITION

Subject Index:

Wilkerson, Shannon

Title: To My Girls – A Look at Friendship from the Perspective of 8 Women

    1. Friendship 2. Motivational 3. Inspirational 4. Women's Issues

Paperback ISBN (2): 978-1-7350703-6-0

shanniwilke.com

Dedication

This book is dedicated to all my good girlfriends, sisters, aunties, cousins and clients. You, your personal journey and our journey together has in some way inspired this book. You are amazing! Keep shining bright!

Table of Contents

Prologue 1

Introduction 3

Chapter One: She Did What?! 5

Chapter Two: Growing Up and The Girls 14

Chapter Three: Bridesmaids 20

Chapter Four: Hindsight is Always 20/20 29

Chapter Five: People Fall Short 36

Chapter Six: In my Flesh and Unimpressed 43

Chapter Seven: Where Are We Going? 49

Chapter Eight: The Push 56

Chapter Nine: Transitioning 64

Chapter Ten: No Place for Competition 70

Chapter Eleven: Snap Out of It! 76

Chapter Twelve: From Crushed to Confident 85

Friendship Prayer 96

Prologue

I have been tremendously blessed to have been surrounded by very positive, supportive women throughout my entire life with whom I have developed very strong bonds. These women are absolutely irreplaceable to me. I have also had experiences with women that were less than encouraging. Fortunately, the residue from those experiences only caused me to pull my loved ones closer and value them even more.

In this book, I will share with you my experiences navigating friendships and learning lessons along the way. My goal is to squash the myth that women can't get along or that we don't support one another. It's more about the circle of women that we choose to give space in our lives and to trust with our hearts.

What better way to express that than to include other talented, women authors to share their personal stories of friendship as well? In this anthology, you will hear from eight women, including myself, each with a unique story to tell. This book is full of moments that will penetrate your heart and cause you to walk, for a moment, in each of our shoes as you will find many scenarios that you will surely relate to.

Get together with your girlfriends, book club, sisters, or whomever you like to chill with, and start discussing the topics shared in the book. Create, develop, and grow your bonds!

Sincerely,

Shannon

Introduction

Recently, I asked myself if adult women still have best friends. I laughed at the thought. It just seemed like a funny thing that I had left in my childhood. That whole BFF thing just seems so far removed from where I am at this stage of life. My friends have jobs, commitments, children, husbands, businesses, responsibilities, etc. Who has the energy to be someone's best friend? That last part was a joke, but honestly, I thought about how busy we all are. I didn't really feel closer to anyone in the way that they could be considered my "best" friend over anyone else. They all added something different to my life in their own unique way, and I value them equally.

Not having a best friend may seem like a bad thing, if you look at it that way, but I choose not to. I have a lot of women in my life who, though they are busy and living their lives, I can count on them. We don't talk on the phone every day like we did when we were kids with less or no responsibility, but if something were to happen to either of us, the world would stop for the other. At any moment, these women would stop what they were doing to be at my side, and I would do the same for them. That makes all of them my best friends.

They have been with me through everything, seen me at my best and my worst and love me anyway. We don't always see eye to eye, but we resolve our issues with no lingering residue of the problem and continue on. We support one another, we encourage one another, and we are there for one another. We have shed both happy and sad tears together through life events, prayed for each other, and genuinely care.

So, no. I don't have a best friend like I did when I was younger and in high school, but I literally have the best friends that I could ever ask for. I don't know if any of them consider me their single most "best friend" in the world, and that's okay. It's not a contest. I just know that there are several people in my corner without question. What more could a person ask for in the friend department?

I hope that you have people like this in your life and that you are this type of friend to them also. Friendship is not about showing up to every event, spending hours on the phone, social media shout outs, or stopping by my house for tea every day like they do on reality shows. Obviously, we do these things when time and life permit, and you should, at some point, make time for your friends to continue to grow your bond. However, what's most important to me is whether you are there when it counts.

    I hope that you will enjoy our book and that it will give a new perspective on forming friendships with other women, being a good friend, and letting go of those who are not really for you and this next phase in your life. I wish you meaningful friendships, unity, and love from your girls!

Chapter One

She Did What?!

My friend, Angela, once sat me down and said to me, "You have to stop taking on people as projects." It immediately sank in. It was like being granted permission to leave people behind that I had been dragging a mighty long way. I had, over time, fallen into these "friendships" with people who were not actually friends to me. They were around for one reason or another, but the goal never seemed to be to reciprocate friendship.

I had been in business for a few years and, through doing business, had connected with a lot of new people on a professional level. In some cases, personal relationships developed, and we became "friends," or so I thought. I had to learn the hard way that not everyone is a friend. Some are opportunists who will flock to you because they see something that they want, and they feel like you are the doorway to that thing.

I was approached by a young lady while working. We will call her Jessica. Jessica was bubbly, full of energy, very friendly, outgoing, and business-minded. So, when she offered to help me with certain business tasks, I was thrilled. I was finally going to be able to delegate some of the things that were robbing me of my time to someone else. Who doesn't want to get some of their time back? I certainly did!

When we met, I had been working as a business coach and had a full list of entrepreneur clients. I was renting office space and meeting with them regularly. I had ideas for taking my business to the next phase and needed a team to get it done. This is what Jessica walked into, and I saw her as a potential part of this team that was in my head. She was very helpful. She didn't always hit the mark exactly, but I appreciated the fact that she was willing to do the work and even bring a few ideas to the table.

We worked together for several months. At some point, she gained open access to me, my brain, and my files. I would soon learn that this was a horrible mistake! Nobody should have as much access as she did unless they are an actual partner in your business who equally contributes. Her little ideas here and there definitely did not qualify. I left myself completely unprotected from this woman that I was kind of still just getting to know, thinking that she had good intentions.

Jessica was introduced to all my clients at networking events that we hosted together, and they came to know her as a part of my team. Everyone felt comfortable with her and trusted that we were on the same team. I knew that she was picking up a lot of tips along the way, and I was okay with that. I had zero issues with her learning all that she could from me so that she could one day do her own thing successfully. I just never thought that she would do so at my expense.

After months of smiling in my face, having lunches, dinners, and sometimes drinks together, sharing details of our lives, and receiving all that I was willing to extend in her direction, she betrayed me! We hosted what I didn't know would be our last event together. During that event, she made a huge deal out of a small thing and got really upset about it. This was totally out of character for the Jessica that I had come to know and super petty. It came completely from left field, and I was definitely caught off guard.

Jessica snapped at me in a way that I had not seen up until that point. Because we were in the middle of an event, I had to let it go and not respond. No argument is worth my professional reputation, and this girl was not going to have me acting a fool in front of my clients and their friends. I walked away from her with grace and continued socializing with my guests, the whole time itching to address the issue with her.

Following the event, Jessica and I never spoke again. A month later, she was running a business exactly like mine. EXACTLY! She even implemented all the ideas that I shared with her. Because my clients knew her as a part of my team, some of them signed up to do business with her, thinking that I was a part of what she was doing. So, she took some of my clients with her temporarily. Once they figured out what was going on, they came right back to me. Always remember that nobody can take what is meant for you unless you give it to them. I strongly believe that, and my life is a testimony to it.

Years later, curiosity got the best of me, and I did some research on Ms. Jessica. That business was a total flop. She was not successful at trying to duplicate my programs. Why? Because there is only one me, and there is a difference between a good idea and a "God idea." God gave those ideas to me to implement. Yes, someone can copy it, but they can't do it like me. I must admit that I laughed to myself upon discovering this failure. It's not that I wished her any hardship. I just knew that her betrayal would not be rewarded, and it hadn't been.

See, I was trying to help Jessica. I wasn't exactly where I wanted to be professionally, but I was further along than she was. I wanted to help her to at least get to my level in hopes that from there, we could grow the business together. I am of the train of thought that together we can achieve more, and I took that approach with her. I thought she and I were on the same page and that she would appreciate my efforts to support her personal and professional growth. I have always been willing to share my knowledge to help someone else to get ahead.

Other women or their success has never threatened me. I've always wanted to see others win! This experience with Jessica did not change that for me. I just learned to be smart about the way I move with new people and how much access they should have at different phases of the relationship. It is impossible for a person to betray me the way that Jessica did because I learned from that one experience. However, my lessons did not stop there. There would be more to come as I navigated through making connections with women in business.

I have met a lot of women being a woman entrepreneur that serves women entrepreneurs. I have learned lessons from almost all of them. Some of these lessons were pleasant experiences, and others were not, but they were all valuable. We've grown and learned from each other.

Exchanges

Most of us have or have had, at some point, varying relationship levels with people. Some are a part of our lives because we are a puzzle piece necessary to get them to the next level in life. They may not at this time or anytime have anything to offer us. Our relationship with them is based on us being able to pour into them. I think that each of us is called to this type of relationship at some point in our lives.

God will use us to elevate and encourage people without expectation of return from the individual. The Bible tells us that *"a great reward awaits you in Heaven,"* Matthew 5:12 (NLT). For me, this means that God is the rewarder. Knowing this, I do not run from these types of relationships. However, this is not what is acceptable in my friendships. In friendships, there should be give and take. I should receive from you just like I give to you.

Now, don't get me wrong. I'm not keeping count of good deeds to see who's doing the most or to judge who hasn't done enough. In a reciprocal friendship, there's just a feeling of security in your bond when this is operating correctly. It's very similar to our romantic relationships. We should have the same expectations and security. Of course, it's way different, but you know what I mean.

The experiences you have with other women are closely linked to who you are as a woman, what you attract to yourself, and what you are willing to deal with. I don't want you to start to feel uncomfortable. So, I'm going to take you out of the hot seat and talk about me. As a teenager and young adult, I wasn't very social with other girls. I was all about my boyfriend and didn't really put in much effort to make girlfriends. I had one friend, Danielle, and I was cool with that. Prior to switching schools and becoming friends with her, I kind of lost contact with some other girls who I was friends with from the old neighborhood and at my old school. I was consumed in my transitions, and our friendships just sort of faded out.

By the time I joined my church as an adult, Danielle and I had also faded out. You know how it is with your high school friendships. There were no issues between us. We just went in slightly different directions, which is typical. At church, I started to socialize with women who I originally met during my childhood at that same church. I slowly started to be open to the idea of letting people in and having girlfriends. For the most part, it was a smooth transition with very few bumps along the way.

Today, almost twenty years later, I still maintain these friendships. They are the most stable bonds in my life outside of my family. I could have had more friends, but it wasn't a priority to me at that point in my life. Even when I joined the church, there were people who I hung out with that seemed to know and be friendly with everyone at the church, and yet I didn't really know these other women. It didn't really bother me, though. I was content with the friends I had. I wasn't super open to other people. I've always preferred a smaller circle, and I saw some things going on in the church that made me kind of want to keep to myself and my small circle.

In my early twenties, I started doing business and met a lot of people who I became friendly with. When you meet friends at church or school, you typically get to know them over a period of years and create an organic bond. This is very different from meeting people out in the "real world." Things get a lot trickier and more complicated. I wasn't ready for it!

Because I wasn't ready for it, people took advantage of my kindness. When you start encountering people from all different backgrounds and walks of life who are not like you at the core as far as your morals and values go, you can run into problems, especially if you think they're going to be like your church friends. Trust me, many people will not approach you from a place of "love thy sister." People have their own motives that don't always immediately surface.

There were people around me who were genuine and poured into me. We made exchanges. Then there were people who wanted to be friends because they saw me as an opportunity, like Jessica. I was a resource that could help them to reach their goals. The "friendship" was counterfeit. They were around because it was beneficial with no intention of benefiting me in any way. I have stories for days; some of them happened recently. This is one of the reasons why I value my friendships so much.

I'm sharing this because I don't want to paint a picture that everyone is for you and that as women, we are all going to link arms and be BFF's. Let's be real. We won't. That would require everyone to let go of their past experiences, conquer their insecurities, and deal with their trust issues. Not everyone will get to that place, but there are certainly enough women who have or are at least working on it for you to form great friendships and have beautiful experiences. I am certainly not going to let the Jessicas of the world change who I am.

Reflection

Often, when we think about moving too quickly in a relationship, we think about romantic relationships. As I just shared, this can also be true in our friendships. Describe a time when you moved too quickly in a friendship or missed the red flags that a friendship wasn't genuine? What happened?

What did you learn from the experience?

Are your friendships one sided? What types of exchanges are happening? Give as many examples as you can think of.

_____

What else came to mind as you read about my experiences and reflected on your own? Did you learn anything about yourself or your friends?

_____

In the next chapter, you're going to meet Toni. I enjoyed reading her story because there were so many similarities to mine, though our experiences were different. It was also fun to read because I was there through most of what she is describing. Toni is my baby sister. I have seen her go through the ups and downs and around in circles with friends as a teen and very young adult. I have also seen her hold onto amazing lifelong friendships. What a blessing to have her to share in this book.

Meet Toni

Chapter Two

Growing Up and The Girls

Growing up with a single mom and two older sisters, I've always been surrounded by women. I was the baby of the house, often looking at my older sisters' relationships with their girlfriends. I always looked up to them, thinking that their lives were so fun. Counting down the days, I couldn't wait to be old enough to hang out at the mall or go to the movies without my mom. I had tons of friendships with the girls in my classes in grade school and throughout middle school. I remember when I had to switch middle schools in seventh grade, and my closest girlfriends had the class sign a t-shirt for me so that I wouldn't forget them after I moved away.

My relationships with women started off pretty good for the most part. Of course, as you enter your teen phase, you may experience little fights with girlfriends here and there and make up by lunchtime or after school. As I got older, I started to notice a shift in my relationships with girls. I often found myself being the new girl in school, and the other ladies weren't always so welcoming.

As much as I wanted to, I didn't make friends easily. With cliques already formed and bonds already made, opening up to the new girl seemed to be a foreign concept to some of the ladies. I thought I was pretty awesome and that the other girls were crazy for not wanting to be friends with me.

Due to my previous relationships with childhood friends, I was very trusting once I became friends with other girls in class. Unfortunately, this did not always didn't turn out so great. This continued up until early adulthood. I made a few lifelong friends along the way, and they would often joke about me always making new friends at work and trusting them so easily. Things would eventually fall off, and I would hear the famous words, "I told you so." I couldn't help it, being around women all the time, I've always been a girl's girl, but in life, I had to learn some tough lessons.

For most of my early 20's, my outlook on women in general was negative. I thought that women would stab you in the front and in the back without thinking twice. This happened especially in the era when social media was becoming more popular. Remember Myspace? It was a huge deal to be in someone's Top 8, even the placement of your top 8 was important. With the click of a button, friendships were ended when someone was removed from the list!

At that point in my life, I thought that women were all about gaining popularity and catfights. I felt like I could no longer be myself with the constant bickering and backstabbing. I had a huge wall up, especially after I found myself constantly ending friendships. I felt like I could no longer be my silly, carefree self without fear that it would be taken advantage of. I couldn't understand why any of this was happening. I was completely done with making new friends. In my eyes, women were the enemy to me.

This was a difficult time, because, in your early twenties, you are figuring out who you are and who you want to be. You are constantly changing and growing as a person and making positive connections with people, especially peers, is a big part of that development. I had been let down and it was affecting my ability to form these connections.

We Either Click or We Don't

Over time, growth, and continued life lessons, I knew that I had to take a step back from my own little world. Everything isn't always going to be gumdrops and rainbows with every woman that you meet. Every woman you come across isn't meant to be your friend, but it doesn't make them a bad person. There came a point when I needed to figure out why my relationships with some women were not turning out to be the best. I had to explore whether there was anything I did or could have done differently to change this.

It takes a great deal of self-reflection to realize that a lot of things could have been handled differently, and not every woman is the enemy. I had to learn that the reality is that everyone isn't going to like you and want to be best friends. Talk about a hard pill to swallow! I had to learn to accept things for what they were and focus more on maintaining the meaningful relationships I developed with some incredible women.

Even with some awful and truly heartbreaking experiences with women, it was always still a good thing to keep in mind that I've had some of the best experiences of my life with some of my best girlfriends. Not only have I had great experiences, but I have also been blessed to have friends who are supportive to me in different ways. Being surrounded by different women from all walks of life, I have learned so much about cultures, lifestyles, and backgrounds.

Through all my great experiences, I can think of one of my best moments with the wonderful women in my life, which involves one of my many business ventures over the years. Growing and learning more about myself, I was trying new things, and one of my ventures was an online boutique. The overwhelming amount of anxiety that I felt with this new venture was something I never felt before. At one point, I even tried to give up before I started.

The women around me were all very supportive. I called my sisters, who always provided support, guidance, and prayer. Some of my best friends answered all my late-night calls and text messages for much-needed pep talks and motivation. The night before my launch, my best friend helped with a last-minute photoshoot of my inventory. The stress was at an all-time high, and often too much for me.

I remember having a celebration dinner to mark the start of my new business the day before my birthday. My best friend planned the dinner. Being surrounded by so much love and support, it was one of my proudest moments, and I am still forever grateful for that moment in my life. As I continue to evolve into who I am as a woman in my 30's, I still receive the same support with new ventures and chapters in my life.

Some of my girlfriends that I have been fortunate enough to have in my life since my pre-teen years remembered when I used to share some of the stories and plays that I wrote. They would get so frustrated with me for never finishing my stories, as they would be so invested in the characters looking forward to what would happen next. I laugh thinking about this because I often began things without finishing, but no matter what, I still received so much support from them.

About two years ago, I told one of my friends that I would write a book. She challenged me to finish it and was so very supportive of my decision to begin doing what I once loved. Of course, I was nervous to start writing again, because it had been so long since I put the things that go on in my mind down on paper. Writing is one of my more personal ventures, but with the proper support and encouragement, I began to write again.

My view on relationships with women now versus the view I held in my 20's has changed tremendously. I realized through life lessons and just plain growth that my relationship and experiences with women are totally based on what I make of them. Everyone is not the same, and every woman is not your enemy. I love that we are now in a time when we see more women embracing, encouraging, and supporting one another, which thankfully, I do not see changing anytime soon.

Women realize that we can learn so much from each other, and when working together, so much can be accomplished. As I look forward to all the amazing people that I know I will come across, I cannot forget all my current relationships with women or those I had in the past. They are all valuable lessons and experiences. Whether good or bad, they have shaped me to be who I am now.

Forever learning, forever growing, and forever evolving.

Reflection

What was your childhood experience with friends like?

_____
_____
_____
_____
_____
_____
_____
_____
_____
_____

How has that shaped how you approach friendships today?

_____
_____
_____
_____
_____
_____
_____
_____
_____
_____

Toni Wilkerson

Growing up, Toni was always a very expressive little girl with a love for writing, singing around the house, or acting with her doll babies. As she got older, she wrote short stories and plays to entertain friends. She is very excited to embark upon this journey as a first-time author and looking forward to future projects. When she is not writing, Toni is busy planning her next trip, reading a good book, catching a new movie, decorating, or spending time with loved ones. She currently resides in Maryland.

Chapter Three

Bridesmaids

When you think of a wedding, what do you think about? I think about a celebration of love surrounded by your closest family and friends who all love and support you individually and as a couple. You pick special people in your life to be in your wedding party, usually your family members, best friends, or a combination of the two. The people who make that list are near and dear to you and are all for your union and new life, right? It doesn't always turn out this way, and this is where friendship can get tricky.

I have had to turn down two invitations to be in the wedding party of "friends." It's never an easy thing to do. It can be a super uncomfortable conversation that usually brings out other things. You know, those underlying issues or the elephant in the room, so to speak. I am the type of person who will not celebrate with you just for the sake of celebration and fun. I won't support or encourage something that I know will harm you in the long run or already has. I know that some people feel as though we should just let adults make their own decisions, but is that true friendship? I think within a friendship, you should be able to speak freely and be heard even if you have an unpopular opinion.

If you are in a domestic violence situation and I am aware, yet I stand next to you at your wedding smiling and congratulating you, am I really being a friend? You may not want to hear what I think about your relationship, but in a case like that, you need to hear it. If you are so blinded by love that you won't protect your safety, should I be blind too?

Well, that was the dilemma I was faced with, and I chose to speak up and decline the wedding party invite. I explained to my friend why I did not support her choice to marry this guy and that I was concerned for her. I knew that this would affect our friendship because I know the nature of people. If a person decides to be in a relationship of any kind with someone others don't approve of, the disapproving person gets cut off. Almost 100% of the time, this is going to be the case, and this was true for us as well.

I was deeply saddened that my longtime friendship didn't recover but stood firm in my decision. She ended up not getting married because more violence followed the invitation, and things ended badly. We just never got back to a good place in our friendship after that. Once things are said, and feelings get involved, some people find it hard to go back to the way things were. I'm sure it was also embarrassing for her. I would never bring it up again, though. That's just the type of friend I am. I will always allow you to be at peace with your mistake and move on from it.

The other time I turned down an invitation to be a part of the coveted wedding party, was with another childhood friend I loved dearly. Though my feelings about her did not change, as we grew from being silly children to adults, our friendship did. Do you know how some friendships are strong, no matter the distance or time? Well, this wasn't one of those types of situations. Distance and time proved to be more than our friendship could handle. Add in becoming adults and being two totally different people, and it's a done deal.

It wasn't really anybody's fault; the friendship just fizzled out. We were close friends as children and off and on friends in early adulthood, but life happened, and we changed. We had not spoken to one another in a long while due to an argument, of which the details I can't even remember. One day after reconnecting, she expressed that she was getting married and would like me to be a bridesmaid. I was caught off guard for sure. I didn't consider us to be as close as we once were and didn't want to be a part of her wedding. I was happy to attend and even bring a nice gift, but bridesmaid seemed like a lot for where we were in our relationship. I just wasn't feeling it. I declined.

That wasn't easy to do because I cared about her and her feelings and didn't want to stunt the progress that we had made in getting reconnected. Still, I would also feel funny about being a part of something so special for someone that I didn't feel connected to in that way. She was a little offended that I said no but got over it. As time continued, more space was created between us. I was okay with that. I am not sure if she ever got married or where she is now, but we are obviously not friends at this point.

I think people like the idea of having certain people around because it looks and feels good to be able to say that you've had this friend since you were three years old. That's very sweet and cute, but let's be real. We weren't even close enough for me to know her fiancé's name. I had no idea who she was marrying, where they had met, how long they had been together, or anything else. I wasn't a part of their lives. I was someone from her past.

Growth spurts often occur in life, not just from childhood or adolescence to adulthood. We are continually growing and changing. I believe we remain the same at our core, but we change in many ways. Some of our friendships won't last through our transformations. That doesn't make either party a bad person or even a bad friend. It just makes them a seasonal friend who was there for a specific time in your life, and that's okay.

There Are Levels to This

In March 2020, things started to shut down, and people were advised to stay in their homes due to a global pandemic. The first couple weeks of being at home were busy for me because I had a lot going on with family and obligations, but I at least spoke to friends via text throughout that time. Around week five, I started to notice some of the people I had been hanging with had not reached out to me even once, no text, no call, no DM, nothing.

This was eye-opening to me. It showed me that these were not friendships. We are simply people who enjoy each other's company and occasionally hang out. That is not a knock at any of them at all because we are still very cool with each other. I just no longer have them in the friend category in my life. I still care for them and will likely still enjoy their company, but we aren't friends, and that is crystal clear to me. A friend would reach out even when there is no happy hour to go to.

Even with my real friends, I have a different relationship with each of them. I vibe with each of them in a very different way. They each know something about me that the others don't know. It's not that I trust one more than the other. I just share with them based on what I think they can relate to or help with. For me, it's about how we connect around a certain topic. I know how each friend will receive certain information, and if their response will be helpful or if they will get on my nerves because they are less open than another friend would be.

The thing to remember is that none of us are perfect. We all have flaws and things about us that will, at some point, rub someone else the wrong way. That's life. You just have to ask yourself if the friendship is worth dealing with the parts of their personality that you don't like. It sounds like I'm talking about a romantic relationship, right? That's because it's very similar.

At this stage in my life, I am just as serious about picking my friends as I am about romantic relationships. They are both special bonds that I enter into with the expectation that it will be a lifetime relationship. Otherwise, why get involved? I don't have space in my life for part-time people in any capacity. I need stability in relationships, all of them! If you are only going to be a business associate, do that consistently. If we are associates who hang out sometimes, that's okay. That's who you are to me.

I don't do gray areas in my relationships. I am very black or white in a way that I wasn't before. Life offers many challenges without us even looking for them, and having a core group of people that you do life with is major. I need those people to be easily identified. I don't want to play a guessing game, and I don't want to find out in a tight spot that people aren't who I thought. I'll pass. "Miss me with that", as they say.

One thing I am not doing at 40 years old that I did when I was younger, is put in a lot of effort into a friendship that is not working. This only positions you to live in drama city until you finally decide to just let go of the friendship. Whenever I have done this in the past, it has always turned out that the person wasn't for me anyway. Now I choose to focus my attention on the relationships in my life that are positive, where I feel loved, and where exchanges are made.

Reflection

Do you agree with my decision to decline wedding party invitations twice? Why or why not?

If in the same situation, would you decline like I did or participate to keep the peace?

BFF Behavior

We all have different rules to life and our relationships. These are my "Absolutely Must Haves" in friendship.

1. Defend me when I am not in the room.

2. Be present.

3. Respect my peace.

4. Tell me I'm wrong when necessary (in private)

5. Pray for me.

6. Pray with me.

7. Always be YOU!

8. Give up the 411 no matter what it is.

9. Don't even think about my current situation or my ex.

What are your absolute must haves in friendship?

1. _____

2. _____

3. _____

4. _____

5. _____

6. _____

7. _____

8. _____

9. _____

10. _____

In these next pages, you are going to learn about Bonnetta's journey through becoming a teenage mom, all the emotions and challenges that accompany that experience, and the support she received from a special person in her life who extended friendship and guidance to her. She also shares her 9-month journey to self-discovery that she embarked upon with a group of women who became friends. I'm sure that many of you will be able to relate and be blessed by her words.

Meet Bonnetta

Chapter Four

Hindsight is Always 20/20

Becoming a mother at seventeen years old was not how I planned to spend my senior year of high school. My friends were celebrating, enjoying their freedom and youth while I was preparing to be responsible for a whole human. Life as I knew it was about to change drastically. It happened overnight. Well, let's be honest, it wasn't overnight, but it was set to change the course of my path.

I was a seventeen-year-old girl, still in high school and living at home. What did I have to offer a child? I went through a plethora of emotions as I racked my brain about the totality of the situation. Have you ever been in a situation where you know how you got there but not really sure how you got there? I was scared, and so was my child's father. We were two scared teenagers embarking on a life-altering journey, blindly and ill-equipped. Can you recall a time in your life when you felt alone, scared, and uncertain of the future or outcome?

More daunting than fear of the unknown was the shame I felt. I wasn't the only girl in high school who was pregnant, but that didn't make it any better. My parents were disappointed and so was I. Can you relate? Have you ever felt like you've let someone down who you love and respect? It's a hard pill to swallow and not at all where I thought I'd be at this phase in my life.

Even scarier was the day we had to inform our parents that they were going to become grandparents in nine months. I had women in my family coming over with their southern rules for how to raise a baby. Their intentions were well placed, but the thought of childbirth became more daunting as they continued to share their hair-raising stories of labor. That was scarier than anything I had ever encountered. I was in a situation where I just couldn't fathom the outcome. I had begun to focus more on the problem than the solution.

I was living in small-town, USA, a place where there was one main street that could get you from the northside of town to the southside in less than five minutes by vehicle. It didn't take long for the news to spread throughout the small community that I was with child. Add on who the child's father was, and people were even more shocked.

It was during this time that I encountered a woman by the name of Mrs. Lena Mae Brown. She is one of the sweetest women I know. She has a kind heart and would give you the last slice of bread in her pantry. She's a wife, mother, grandmother, and loves God. For a seventeen-year-old girl, that was plenty enough reason for me to admire Mrs. Brown.

We were spending time outside one summer day when I approached her. I remember being more nervous than normal. She could detect that I had important news to share. When my mouth did finally open, all I could muster up was a loud booming sob. It's as though she knew my heart was troubled. I didn't engage much during our conversation. She comforted me, a weary, frightened girl. She boldly instructed me to raise my head, dry my tears, and love the child that was growing in my womb. She sternly said to me the world was not going to end because I was pregnant, and worse things could be happening right now. Can you think of a time you were afraid to share and prepared yourself for the worst response? It can be a challenge but be encouraged.

Mrs. Brown would take me under her wing, sharing stories of how challenging it was to grow up in the south, how important it was to respect elders, give without expectation, and always keep God first. Even if we differed from those around us, she made certain not to highlight those differences, but to embrace them and think outside the box in all relationships.

We would share conversations over sweet tea and homemade pound cake in front of the television watching one of her favorite shows, In the Heat of the Night with one of her favorite actors, Howard E. Rollins. At the time, it would have been impossible to know the depth of how she played an intricate part of my life. Her piece to the puzzle of my life mattered. Although it wasn't the entire pie, it was the piece that set me on a course for success in my future relationships with women.

Although she wasn't obligated to, Mrs. Brown showed a young girl from small-town USA to respect others and judge not. I was taught these values at home, but she taught me to view it from a different perspective. I learned how to be compassionate. A new mother and still just a child myself at the time, I could use all the advice anyone had to offer.

I recall one day; I was experiencing pain in an unusual area while pregnant. It was unfamiliar and scary. I inquired of my best friend's mother, and she assured me it was normal and there was nothing to fear. One of my aunts had laid it all out for me about labor and what I could expect. If you are a mother, I'm sure you can relate to pre-labor jitters. I know I was clueless about what was to come. Sure, I had taken a biology course in high school and was fully aware of human nature, but nothing prepared me for what was to come. I took it all in. I absorbed as much information as I could. I was so blessed to have so many women pour into me and prepare me to give birth to my child. Their words of encouragement and even the hard truth made a huge difference.

A Remarkable Journey

The day I decided to join one hundred women on a personal nine-month, intensive journey of self-discovery and purpose was one of the scariest days of my life. Life had thrown me curveballs, and I thought it was time for me to peel back the layer from my experiences, I wanted to discover who I was at my core and get a peek at whom I would become.

During this journey, I was met with warm smiles and heartfelt hugs. I'll admit I was taken aback and responded to their genuine welcome with much reservation. What was it about this group of women that set them apart? Had they cracked the secret code of sisterhood? Whatever it was, I knew I wanted to be connected to the tribe.

Most women have survived several life-altering events that either shape or break them or break them to shape them, I should say. Initially, I shied away from such social settings, but I knew it was time to confront the thing that was holding me back. In my case, it was having a lot of insecurities hidden beneath the surface. I was distrusting of other women, and judgmental if I'm being honest. What made me feel the way I felt about other women? Have you ever had those thoughts that women are not to be trusted? Well, I was about to be proven wrong on a major scale.

It can be hard to trust people after you've been hurt. We've all been there. But what if you could trust women and work well with them and build together? I had to release my inhibitions and insecurities and go full speed ahead if I was going to learn how to trust women and build meaningful relationships. When doubt started to creep in, I would have a flashback of a conversation with Mrs. Brown. Her words echoed in my heart to highlight whatever differences we shared but to embrace them and think outside the box in all relationships, which included other women.

If I was going to get free so I could be used to inspire and encourage other women, I knew I had to get free in my heart so I could serve in my purpose. What if Mrs. Brown had decided that she didn't have time to show a scared, seventeen-year-old unwed girl how to trust, show compassion, and be open to change. One conversation changed the direction in which I was going. Now along the way, I bumped my head a few times, and her words weren't always present in my heart, but they echoed when I was open to change my views on relationships with other women.

I spent nine months of intense soul searching in prayer, fasting, and seeking God. I hadn't kept Him first for quite some time. Things were about to change for the better. Time spent with Mrs. Brown was the foundation that enabled me to walk this 9-month journey with other women. I had to take people out of boxes and stop judging the book by the cover. Things are not always what they seem.

When the journey ended, I had a better understanding of who I was and how it was my responsibility to reach back and help the next woman. There are several reasons we should support and empower other women. We can be role models for others. Show the women in your life how you overcame an obstacle without tearing another woman down.

We do not have to become what we have learned and see in the media in this ever-changing world we live in. Have you ever heard the saying, "Be the change you want to see?" We can create cultural change right now. There is truth in the statement, "There is strength in numbers." We are better together. We will achieve more if we support, love, affirm, encourage, motivate, and edify one another.

Mrs. Brown would encourage me to use my voice. I'll admit I would use my voice, but it wasn't always for the right reason or right time. Will you choose your words to build another woman up? Your words have power. But since I learned to love myself, free my heart from its hardened condition, supporting other women became second nature.

I had to scrub out the old and allow the good in so I could have genuine relationships. We are better equipped to assist others once we ourselves are healed. I take pleasure in helping other women achieve their goals. I love to see others win. I can recall a time when my junk got in the way of seeing others win. Now, I rejoice when others rejoice. The gratitude is immeasurable once you realize that you possess the capability to help another woman achieve her goals. Your words of affirmation, encouragement, and support will go far beyond the person you assisted. You will ignite the next woman to go further, push harder, dream bigger, and believe she possesses what it takes to do so. Do you see how that works? Even if you can't unearth their strengths or talents, you can help spark them and steer them in the right direction.

Our power is limitless! Let us continue to build one another up and soar!

Reflection

What have you had to overcome?

_____
_____
_____
_____
_____
_____
_____
_____
_____
_____
_____

Who was part of that journey with you?

_____
_____
_____
_____
_____
_____
_____
_____
_____
_____
_____

Bonnetta Petties-Simmons

Bonnetta Petties-Simmons is a "people-lover" at heart. She was born and raised in Southern Illinois but resides in Maryland with her family. She has been in the medical field much of her career but left to pursue her love and passion for writing in which she is pursuing a degree in English Literature. She uses her gifts and talents to encourage and empower other women to live their best life. When she isn't writing, you might find her enjoying museums, walks or traveling with her family.

Chapter Five

People Fall Short

A comment that was made on a popular reality tv show recently really stuck with me. Two friends were having a moment of coming back together after several situations that compiled to cause a rift in their relationship. As they were both saying their apologies, one of them acknowledged that she had fallen short in the friendship department. She went on to explain that she didn't really know how to be a friend. She only knew how to fight. She made reference to coming from nothing, being told that she wouldn't ever be anything and feeling like she had to work even harder to prove people wrong. She said that because of this, she, at times, can be so caught up in her own life that she forgets about checking in with other people.

This really got my attention because it opened my eyes to where and how I may fall short in friendship. Like her, I am very goal focused. Sometimes to the point that I can get consumed by the goal. That can be a good thing as relates to accomplishing what you set out to do, but a bad thing for relationships. I don't want that to ever make me emotionally unavailable to connect to the people in my life.

I'm not great with life balance. I will be the first to admit that. When I am working on something, it has my full attention. I have had friends upset with me because I didn't come to their birthday party or baby shower. In my mind, these things shouldn't be major. That's because they aren't major to me. I had to realize that they are major to other people. I felt like people should understand that I have a deadline and just accept the gift before or after the event and keep it moving. Not all my friends feel that way, and I had to make adjustments. This doesn't mean that if you have seven baby showers that I will be at each one, but I try.

As a super driven person who is always moving on to the next thing, it is important for me to check in on my relationships to keep them healthy, not just afloat. Our relationships should be better than just not sinking. That shouldn't be how you measure the success of your relationships. We must pour into them what we want to receive back, but also what our friends need from it. That may look very different from what we personally need.

Finding balance can be a struggle for a lot of people, and it heavily depends on what motivates you. I can't say that I came from nothing, but I didn't come from a lot. That is not the lifestyle that I wanted to continue in, and that is not what I want for my children. So, I am motivated by my definition of success. What success looks like for me may not be what it looks like for you. I personally did not want to live in rented property my whole life. I wanted to give my future children a home that they could come back to and later own when I am gone. I did not want to live a lifestyle of pinching pennies. I wanted to be able to manage all my bills without giving it a second thought and to splurge when I felt like it, not when I got a bonus check. With those two big goals in mind came hundreds of smaller goals that each requires a certain level of focus, time, and attention. There were times when this interfered with my social life. This was a sacrifice I knew I had to make, but I didn't want to sacrifice my friendships.

Maybe there is something else that motivates you that takes up a lot of your energy and headspace, leaving very little room for your relationships. Check that! Nothing should consume us to the point of not being able to nurture our bonds. There is a major difference between having regular responsibilities and obligations that may give us a little less time to just hang with the girls and totally neglecting your friendships.

Be patient with your friends who are sometimes absent. Often, people struggle with things consuming them that are not necessarily their choice. You likely have a friend who suffers from depression, anxiety, alcoholism, and a variety of other things that you may know nothing about. People closest to us will still hide the most embarrassing things about themselves out of fear of being shamed or looked at differently. Nobody wants to flaunt their flaws in front of others. We can only hope that we are close enough for them to feel comfortable sharing that part of themselves with us.

It Takes 2

We love to think that we are perfect. Every falling out is the other person's fault, we always give our all to everyone, and everyone else in the world is wrong. If you add on top of that at least one person who is willing to agree and take our side, you can't tell us anything. We are perfect angels who never fall short, right? Sooo wrong! Of course, I am exaggerating, but nobody likes to be at fault or to admit playing a role in the downfall of a thing. However, it takes two to make a thing go right, and it also takes two to make a thing go wrong!

One beautiful thing about friendship that I love is that it is forgiving. Our friends are near and dear to our hearts. We love them like we love our family. Because of this great fondness, making right a wrong is usually as simple as just apologizing. The thing about apologizing is that it requires a person to look at themselves and acknowledge wrongdoing. Most of us have been taught by well-intended people to protect and defend ourselves at all costs, especially those of us who grew up in kind of rough circumstances. We were taught that out of love. Our parents, aunties, uncles, big brothers, etc. didn't want to see us being taken advantage of or harmed in any way by others. That is all very understandable, and that teaching has probably gotten us through some of life's situations coming out on the winning end. However, that hard exterior is like poison to heart relationships.

Our friendships are heart relationships. We tell our friends all our business, we cry together and celebrate each other. We aren't like that with just anybody, only those with whom we have heart connections. Treat them as such. The same way a spouse shouldn't be working to break down the layers of your heart five years into the relationship, neither should your friends. Stop being that way! If someone has proven themselves tried and true, let down your guard, be vulnerable, admit that you aren't perfect.

We live in a day and age where the images of friendship that we see are so surface level and not based on anything other than a real need to be associated with one another for whatever reason. In some cases, the only reason is to compete with one another. Everyone is putting up a front pretending to be one thing when in real life, it's a whole other thing. How can you make a real connection being fake?

On reality television, everyone pretends to be friends just to be a part of the mix. The more you watch, the more your view of relationships with other women will be skewed. TV will have you thinking that friendship is about meeting up for drinks to talk about other people's business or to gang up on a woman the two of you have agreed not to like. Then the moment one friend does something that the other doesn't like, she becomes the next victim. The sad part is that there are grown women who base their friendships on some of the same things and seeing those images on television only deepens the craziness of it all. As adult women, we have to be about more than this. What happened to women supporting women? Can we get back to that? If this is an area where you have fallen short, and you are willing to admit it to yourself, it is time to change some things.

One thing that I am truly certain of is that if you show yourself friendly, you will have true friends. Not friendly in the sense that you smile at people and make small talk, but in the way that you are a good friend to those around you. We typically receive back the same energy that we give. This can either work for or against you. Which do you prefer?

Reflection

How easy is it for your loved ones to come to you to apologize?

_____
_____
_____
_____
_____
_____
_____
_____
_____
_____

Are you forgiving or do you hold things against them? Why?

_____
_____
_____
_____
_____
_____
_____
_____
_____
_____

Write a note to a friend you need to apologize to.

Next, you are going to meet Latoya, a dear friend of my sister who became a friend to our family. The power of connection is an awesome thing, and I am so honored to have her share her experiences in this book. She is very relatable. You may even find this chapter a bit humorous as you see yourself through her story.

Meet Latoya

Chapter Six

In my Flesh and Unimpressed

I can remember the day so vividly, right down to the detail of the clothing we were wearing. Image after image playing through my mind so clearly, it's as if I were reliving it and not simply relying on my mind's recall. The Pastor had pulled me into the office to admonish me for my not-so-subtle dislike for the new visitor. While she was "new" to our church, she certainly wasn't new to me. Nothing pronounced had happened between the two of us, but she was "best friends" with a young lady who I wouldn't refer to as a "best" anything. That fact alone caused me to turn the other cheek and cross the room anytime "Dominique" was nearby. He began by reminding me, "The bible says we must cast a net far and wide…" admittedly something that had always given me pause. We were a small church and a well-acquainted group, a nice fit. Not yet of one mind and one accord, but we got along well enough on Sundays and Thursdays. Knowing full well where he was going with it I respected Pastor enough to turn my head before rolling my eyes as he continued; "I know that Sister Dominique is not your favorite person, but she is really considering joining this church, and I don't want that hindered by you not getting along with her."

    I winced at what was being implied. Could my lack of fondness really be a factor in someone not seeking to further their relationship with God in a church home? The answer is yes. The world is cruel and cold, distant, and yet still all too near. If you're getting beat up out there in the world, the last thing you expect is to come into the house of the Lord and receive coldness, among other things. "Well, that shouldn't affect someone's decision if they're not there for you but are there for God," some would say. Consider the fact that plenty of people have left well-paying jobs for which they have tenure to avoid conflict, and for peace of mind. I know this because I was once forced to make that decision.

So, for some, especially those who are already a recipient of church hurt or wavering in their faith, it does matter.

I recovered from the sting of the Pastor's words and agreed that no, the church is not the place to express your disinterest in a person. Additionally, during the lesson about love, I realized that I barely even knew Dominique. My feelings against her were based solely on the fact that she was friends with someone who I was at odds with. It didn't help that the feeling was mutual. She didn't really like me either.

After a few more minutes of discussion, Pastor asked me to give him my word that I would turn the page on this chapter of our lives, and I promised then and there that I wouldn't let this situation interfere with her joining our church family. I vowed not to be the reason someone didn't choose our church as a home and decided to get to know her and allow her the opportunity to get to know the real me.

Walking in Love and Light

The words of my proclamation came out so easily, flowing like the words of one of my favorite songs. It felt good to let the negativity go that day. Next, it was time for some action, and that proved to be a bit more difficult. The high from Sunday's service had begun to wear off, and life started happening. Just dealing with the start of the work week nearly made me forget I'd made the proclamation in the first place. While my heart was in the right place to forgive and forget, my mind was a harder sell.

Experience helps shape and form our decisions, and because of the things that I've been through, my guard was up, impenetrable. I felt like I wasn't going to allow any new hurt, so no new friends. In doing this, I felt as though I'd won, as if I'd figured out the secret to a happy drama-free life. I alone had broken the code to everlasting happiness; shut everyone out and don't let anyone in. However, there are few greater things than the bond you have with a good friend.

Surely the Pastor, First Lady, and Elders are always available to talk to. However, that isn't the same as calling your good friend because there's no code-switching with him or her. You can keep it 100, vent, laugh, talk, and build. Sisterhood is a true winding road full of sharp turns, potholes, and uncertainties (Alexa, find a Map!), but truly rewarding once you've navigated all of that to reach your next destination.

Bearing that in mind, I made a pointed effort to chat more often with Sister Dominique. I'd find my way over to her just after service or during the break, planting seeds. Neither one of us is big on long hugs or warm embraces, but I did make it a point to speak with her. I admitted I did not take the time to know her before determining that I didn't like her, which was wrong. She respected my honesty and was on board with getting to know each other, and we ended that exchange with plans for a new start and a warm embrace. With that, a connection, sisterhood, and bond was formed that would pave the way for support, opportunity, and growth.

Sister Dominique and I began to work closely at the church resulting in more fellowship functions and a boost in church morale for the kids and adults alike. While rushing to breakdown and clean up a Pastor's appreciation event, Dominique mentioned that she was going to school for her real estate license. I immediately began praying for her and became her cheerleader. I pushed her, gave encouraging words, smiled on the days she frowned and offered a listening ear when it all felt like it was too much. After several attempts, she passed her test, and we celebrated that victory together!

What did either of us gain from me rolling my eyes at her as she entered a room? Nothing! What fulfillment would have come from our high school stance of not liking each other because I didn't get along with her friend? On the contrary, what did we gain from being mature and putting petty pride aside? Growth.

I learned that not everyone is like the women I've dealt with in the past who have disappointed or hurt me. It enhanced my overall mood to walk into the room and share a genuine smile with my sister in the Lord. That was much more beneficial than ignoring her and mustering the energy to be angry every time I saw her. It confirmed the old adage that I follow to this very day, "Treat people the way you want to be treated." I want respect and honesty, and by putting that out, I was able to receive that in return, tenfold. It showed that we are not "angry black women," nor do we need to be to garner respect. We reinforced the fact that together we stand tall and highlighted how important it is to fix another Queen's crown when she's down.

The code that I was following and thought I needed was to shut everyone out. However, I didn't consider why God wanted that person in my life. I was trying to choose my destiny when really my success is being defined by my steps, which are ordered by the Lord. Sister Dominique and I are now working on eating healthy and being fit together. We're working on branding and promoting together as budding entrepreneurs. Having passed the real estate exam and still learning, Dominique is helping me to work towards owning my first home.

What I realized is the things I endured in the past were built by design to make me stronger and wiser and to equip me so that I could see what was coming and recognize it sooner. While I was initially not open to new bonds and friendships worrying only about the past, I almost missed important connections along the way to my future. These connections helped to reveal necessary steps for growth and now top earning potential. I learned not to underestimate the potential of a simple connection with the sister across from, in front, or behind me at my next event.

Reflection

Have you ever had to check yourself about your thoughts or actions towards another woman? Is it necessary to do even right now today?

_____
_____
_____
_____
_____
_____
_____
_____
_____
_____

Was it hard for you to get out of your emotions and be open to the other person? Why or why not?

_____
_____
_____
_____
_____
_____
_____
_____
_____
_____

LaToya Mack

LaToya Mack is a Maryland native and mother of two. A makeup enthusiast at heart, when she isn't writing she spends her time perfecting her craft, having seafood feasts with her friends, or out at the Annapolis and Baltimore waterfronts. Her ideal evening is a rainy night spent at home with her children cooking and dancing.

Chapter Seven

Where Are We Going?

When you decide to connect with someone as a friend, it's usually because you have a shared interest. That could be attending the same church or school, a love for thrift shopping, live music festivals, etc. That shared interest is typically what connects you and gives you activities to do together that you both enjoy. That's cool, but not enough to keep you connected. When it comes to our lifestyle, we also tend to want to be around people with whom we have a lot in common. We like to be at least on the same playing field or headed in the same direction as our friends. This gives you the ability to connect on a deeper level beyond the initial shared interest that connected you in the first place.

This doesn't mean that if you're single, all your friends have to be single. However, I would say that you need some single friends. I'm single and so are most of my friends, most likely because I relate better to them. The same applies to married people. Most married people I know hang around other married folks, and I think that is a good thing. They can learn and grow together as married couples.

We don't have to look for ourselves in other people and only connect with those who are just like us, but we do need to share some core things that make us who we are. Otherwise, there is a lot of space for conflicts and disagreements that go beyond just being able to be mature about a thing and agreeing to disagree. Who has time for that? That type of relationship takes away from you and brings stress. I try to keep life as simple as possible, with no drama attached to my relationships.

Have you ever found yourself in a religious debate with someone? It is the most tiring conversation ever! I had to learn to not feed into this type of thing. Now, once I see where it's going, I immediately hop right out of that conversation. Because my beliefs are a major part of who I am, I tend to be more attracted to friendships with people who share my beliefs. It allows me to not only have fun on vacations or at the mall with my friends but also to worship with them. That is a beautiful thing that I value so much. I have a few friends who believe differently, but we aren't as close, and I refuse to have discussions about religion with them. It's a topic that we don't touch. I try to keep our time together focused on things that we both enjoy, and that's it.

What about the more subtle things that we encounter when choosing friends and developing relationships? Those are the tricky ones because sometimes they sneak up on you. If you are a very goal-focused go-getter, you don't need a friend who is a "Negative Nancy." She will always be in your ear telling you this or that won't work or won't be successful. Depending on how much time you spend with this person, she may even cause you to back off your vision and get off track. Steer clear of people with no vision for their lives because they will slowly but surely eat away at yours. They don't do it to be malicious. It's just who they are. They can't help themselves.

I am so completely unattracted to people who aren't doing anything with their lives. These are the type of people you can love and pray for from a distance. You may not even notice how their presence affects you and your mental state. You'll just notice over time how you start to think and feel differently and become less productive if you don't distance yourself. Its like poison.

You must surround yourself with people who will encourage, uplift, and add to you, as I said before. These people are truly priceless in your life. They keep me going through prayer and sometimes just a quick pep talk. I can literally have a conversation with a friend and leave that conversation feeling energized and ready to take on the world.

Running a business has been, for me, the most rewarding thing, but also the most challenging and sometimes stressful. That's why I always say that entrepreneurs need friends who are entrepreneurs. They can understand better where you are and what you are aiming to accomplish. They are familiar with your unique set of challenges. Your other awesome friends can still support and encourage you, but not from the standpoint of true understanding, and that is what every business owner needs.

When it comes to my own personal friends, they don't all understand everything that I experience, but they can still pray for me. We have that core similarity. I don't see everything the way they see it. We don't always agree. We aren't living inside one brain. We are different. However, at our core, we are a true friendship match. I don't have to question their character, conduct, intentions, or motives because I know who they are, and we are headed in the same general direction, which is working to be our best possible self and creating the life we desire.

The Table

Think about the last potluck dinner you attended. Most people brought something to contribute to the meal. One person brought paper goods, and you kind of rolled your eyes at them because you know they can cook, but they were being lazy. Another brought paper goods, and that was okay with you because you know she really can't cook all that well. Most people contributed something to eat, some side items and some main dishes. Someone even showed up completely empty-handed, but with to-go containers.

Now, think about this in terms of friendships and the people that you have or will encounter. Some will contribute just enough to not look bad, some will go all out, and some will contribute absolutely nothing, but take all they can get. What type of meal is that? There's not enough to go around. So, somebody is leaving hungry. The people who went all out will feel taken advantage of and resent those who didn't. The person who brought just enough to not look bad will wonder why people are upset about that.

In both scenarios, it would have been helpful to be specific. You must tell people what your expectation is. The dinner host could have said everyone must bring a food item or everyone bring sides, and the host will bring the main dish. If no instructions are given, and no expectations have been set, you may end up with multiple dishes of macaroni and cheese. As a friend, you must let it be known what you expect from the friendship, and you don't have to wait until there's an issue and emotions are involved.

As a friend, I expect you to defend me when I am not around, always have my best interest at heart, be honest about everything, correct me when I'm wrong, and support me when I need it. Your friendship needs may look very different from mine, and that's okay. They are yours. Whatever it is, communicate it and ask your friends what they expect. It doesn't have to be a weird conversation. A lot of this you already know from different things that you have experienced together during your friendship.

If you want to connect with other women as a friend, you have to bring yourself to that table, period. Nobody likes one-sided relationships. In a friendship, both parties must contribute who they are. If who you are isn't pleasing to the other person, they will decide not to pursue a friendship, and you can move on to find your circle, again, that's okay. When you find your circle, put who you are on the table. Be genuinely you.

You'll know when it's just not your circle. When the vibe is just not right, you feel like you're the only one putting anything into it, or you just don't enjoy a person's company. I don't waste a lot of time in this place. I stick people in the associate category and keep it moving. I'm too old to hang on to people who I don't need in my life or those who don't want me in theirs, and that applies to all relationships. In my 40 years, I have been there and done that and not only have the t-shirt, but I have the scars too. It's hardly ever worth it. Please learn to walk away from people who aren't connected to your future. It is so important that your friends fit into the master plan for your life.

Someone not being your cup of tea doesn't have to be a bad thing and doesn't have to make the two of you enemies. This is where maturity plays a role. So many times, I have witnessed grown women acting ugly towards another woman just because she's not her favorite person. As a woman, you should be able to be in someone's presence who you are not all that cool with and still be respectful and cordial at the least. Being immature and giving her the cold shoulder is super childish, and it is even worse when you try to get other people to not like her too. Ladies, we have to move past that. We must accept that someone we don't particularly care for, may be an excellent friend to one of our friends and may occasionally be in our presence. Let them have their friendship! You don't have to be a part of it, and they don't need you throwing salt on it either. What they each bring to the table may be what the other needs. It's not your business. You have to be really mature for this, though.

Reflection

Evaluate YOU! Are you bringing your whole self to the table in your friendships? If not, why, and how can you change that?

I enjoyed reading this next chapter because Tylisha talks about mentorship between women. You just don't see much of this anymore. A lot of people with any special skill that others may find valuable simply create a course and charge people to share their knowledge. There is nothing wrong with having an entrepreneurial mind and making your passion pay you. However, there should also be some time set aside to just help someone. Wanting your "sister" to succeed and playing a role in that process is extremely rewarding and I was happy to learn of Tylisha's story.

Meet Tylisha

Chapter Eight

The Push

I joined this project to highlight some of the women who have supported me throughout my journey. These women probably don't even realize just how much of an impact they have had on my life. Marie, the first woman I want to mention, gave me the opportunity to make a name for myself in the hair industry. She gave me the push I needed to fulfill one of my childhood dreams. I always wanted to become a cosmetologist, and to meet one who is considered one of the best in town, felt like meeting a celebrity.

In the town I lived in before moving to Salisbury, MD, in 1991, you didn't see a lot of black hair stylists. I learned so much just watching her style other clients' hair. It was a total transformation from when they walked into the salon. They walked out with a different attitude. When I would go to the salon for my appointment, I loved watching Marie doing different styles. It ignited my burning desire to become a cosmetologist even more.

At the end of my ninth-grade year, when it was time to choose the vocational program that I wanted to pursue the following school year, the choice was obvious. I applied for cosmetology and checked the mailbox everyday for my schedule to arrive, to see if I was selected for the class. Finally, the schedule arrived. I just knew my classes were set, cosmetology class here I come. I opened the letter, and right then, my goal to become a cosmetologist came to a screeching halt. I DIDN'T GET IN! I couldn't understand why! I had the grades, my GPA was a 3.7, and I signed up early enough to be chosen. I needed to figure out what happened.

When I spoke with my guidance counselor, the answer she gave me was unbelievable. I didn't get into the program because the counselor felt that my grades were "too good" to take up a trade. My heart was totally crushed, but my dream didn't die. I knew that somehow; I would still pursue this dream and succeed. I also knew that Marie was the person to help me.

My visits to the salon were always exciting and interesting. Not only did Marie know exactly what to do with my hair without me saying anything, she could also pick up on it when something was going on with me. That's one of her amazing gifts from behind the chair. When I explained how I was bummed about not being chosen for the cosmetology program at Vo-Tech, Marie encouraged me to not let it get me down. She told me to keep pushing to reach my dream. So, I continued doing hair for my friends & family and held onto hope.

The summer before my senior year, I received one of the biggest surprises of my life. I was pregnant! At age 17, I was going to become a mother. With that in mind, I had to focus on graduating high school, and our future. I knew that this would slightly change my plans of becoming a cosmetologist, at least temporarily. I knew that I would have to put that aside for a while and get a job to provide for my baby. I was more than willing to do that for my child.

My son was born in November of 1995. Six months later, I graduated with my baby boy in the audience, yelling mommy. That was one of the greatest feelings in the world. My life was not just my own. I now had a little man that depended on me for everything. I was determined to be the best possible version of myself for him. Graduating high school was only the first step. I knew there was more to come.

In April of 1997, I married my high school sweetheart. At 19 years old, I was a wife and mother. A year later, I gave birth to my second son. Now, my plans had to include not just my dreams, but the needs of three other people. My husband was in the military at the time. So, I knew there would be a time I would be leaving to be with him. However, I also wanted to not only be a cosmetologist but also to work directly under Marie. I knew that she was the best and being able to work with her would be great for my career.

The Process

In August 2001, we were blessed with our third son. Around that time, I found out my department at work was going to be moving to China. I remember talking to Marie, and she told me not to give up. I would just have to attend a private school to get my cosmetology license. One day, I came home and told my husband that I was going to take the severance pay and enroll in the DelMarVa Beauty Academy. That was the best decision I could have ever made for my family. I'm here to tell you that if you have a dream, never give up on it. The time will come when you can fulfill it, no matter how long it takes!

After classes at the beauty academy, I would go to the salon to help Marie. I wanted to absorb all the teaching I could, because her salon was going to be my home once I graduated. I wanted to be the best and I knew that this meant that I had to learn from the best. When class started, there were 20 people enrolled. However, by graduation day, I was the only one in the entire class that was walking. I completed my 1500 hours in the allotted time frame. Next up was the State Board Exam. Of course, I passed on the first try!

All the late nights of studying, the long hours, and the extra help I was getting, paid off. It was time for me to make a name for myself. A lot of people told me that I would not make it at the salon where I chose to work. This was because the head stylist was the best in the town, and everyone wanted to sit in her chair. What they didn't know was that she wanted me to succeed more than anyone. So, the new clients that came in were sent to me, and I started filling my books with appointments. Yes, it was scary, but I knew with God's help, I could do anything I put my mind to. Six months later, I became an Independent Contractor. Not because I wanted to, but because she saw something in me that I didn't see in myself. I truly thank her for the process I went through. You don't find too many salons that will open their doors to new stylists without a clientele base.

Throughout the years working in the salon, I went through a difficult time in my marriage. We ended up getting a divorce in 2012. Marie was right there, helping me pick up the pieces. I wasn't just a stylist that worked in her salon; I was family. That's what made it even more difficult to walk away when I determined that I needed a different job to better provide for my boys as a single parent. Fortunately, I was still able to do hair on the side at my house. I had a passion for styling hair and could not just leave it completely. However, working out of my home was becoming a bit overwhelming. After a while, I had a talk with my family, and in 2013 decided to go back to the salon on the weekends.

During this time, I was reminded that my children were blessed with the most awesome godmothers in the world and that I could lean on them when needed. I couldn't write this chapter and not mention Darnette and Dynette. They knew my motivation to get back to the salon, and they also knew my situation being a single mom trying to make ends meet. When my oldest son graduated high school and got accepted to college, he needed to get supplies for his dorm. They wanted to help make sure he had everything, so they took him on a shopping spree and got everything he needed and more. God placed these ladies in my life to push me and to love me when I felt overwhelmed. These two have been my biggest supporters. I really don't want to know how my life would be without them in it.

There came a time when I met and started working at a salon with LaShonda. God placed her in my life at the right time. When she decided to open her own salon, she asked me if I would like to come and work there with her. She gave me a new place to call home and welcomed my clients and I with open arms. When I first started working with her, my boyfriend would walk up and down the street, handing out my flyers and business cards. She would always tell me, "He is a keeper." You know what, she was right. We were married on January 28, 2016. LaShonda was the first person that knew besides my immediate family.

Two days after our first anniversary, we faced devastating news. My husband had cancer. I knew what I needed to do. I took some time off to take care of my husband. Sadly, my husband lost his battle with cancer in October 2017. Each of the mentioned ladies, were by my side through this experience when I needed them the most. Their support meant so much to me and really helped me make it through one of the most difficult times in my life.

Today in 2020, all my sons are out of school and doing well. Thank God! I have been a Cosmetologist for 17 years, and I am still loving it! I am grateful for the support these women have given me because there was a time I was going to walk away from it all. I am a virtuous woman, and so are all of you. Keep pushing your vision and trust the process!

YOUR DREAM IS SO WORTH IT, AND SO ARE YOU!

Reflection

Did you have someone to mentor you? If so, think about the impact that it had on your life. If you have not, think about how having one could have made things different for you in a particular area.

_____
_____
_____
_____
_____
_____
_____
_____
_____
_____
_____

Write the names of 5 people whom you could potentially mentor. Then reach out to them to see if they are open to the idea.

1. _____
2. _____
3. _____
4. _____
5. _____

Tylisha Cutler-Hagood

Tylisha Cutler-Hagood, age 42, was born and raised on the Eastern Shore of Maryland. She's a class of 1996 graduate of James M Bennett Senior High School, as well as a 2004 Graduate from the DelMarVa Beauty Academy. Tylisha has been a cosmetologist for 17 years and loves what she does, which is, "Enhancing the beauty within you." She's a member of several women empowerment groups. A proud member of New & Living Way Ministries. Tylisha decided to launch her own Widows Empowerment non-profit "Life After This, (A Widow's Story)", after the loss of her husband in Oct of 2017. She's also an entrepreneur, UPSTAGE Bling Boutique & Chino Stylezs, and now she's an author. With everything that she has accomplished so far, still nothing will ever compare to the titles she holds dear to her heart. She is the proud mother of three handsome young men--Tre'Vonte, Tra'Velle, and Ty'Trelle. In 2018, she was blessed to take on the title of "GiGi" to her grandson Karter followed by her granddaughter Brielle only 3 months later. Now, her world is complete.

In life we go through many transitions and phases as we grow and mature as a woman. Farrah's story reflects that and how other women in her life were there to guide her in her journey. It speaks to knowing who you are and being comfortable with her and evolving. It demonstrates our need to belong and to have people in our lives who we connect with and find support in.

Meet Farrah

Chapter Nine

Transitioning

In 2010, I left the military completely and became a civilian. I was a single mother and wanted the freedom to raise my son without being concerned about deployment. At the time, I thought it was the best decision for me. A short time after my separation from the military, I found myself struggling financially, with no job, on welfare, and going to school full time. Many people were not aware of this, but for several months I had to live in someone else's home. I would hear people around me say things like, "You are a Christian, you shouldn't be going through things like this."

After months of living with someone, I moved into my own place on a student's income. During this transition period, I would hear in my spirit, "You need to dress more like a girl." At the time, I was confused, and my response was, "What do you mean, I am a girl? How is a girl supposed to dress?" It wasn't until later that I realized what it all meant. I needed to dress more professionally and business-like for the level God was leading me to. I needed to be more polished.

Soon after, I landed my first government job. I was finally able to financially support my son and purchase new clothes. The same people that were saying to me, "You are a Christian, you shouldn't go through things like that," are the same people who told me I was dressing differently for a man's attention. In reality, a man had nothing to do with the changes that I was making and found necessary for my success.

I knew it was best for me to separate myself from those negative people, their thoughts, and mindset. I knew I needed to do whatever it took to become a better me. So, as I transitioned to becoming, who God called me to be, I had to surround myself with people who encouraged and edified me. Once I sought out this type of people, God started to place them in my life.

The Transition to Better

In order to change who I was, I had to end friendships with people who were negative towards me and those who had misconceptions about me that they believed. I isolated myself and focused on me. It was during this time that I met two women who poured into me both spiritually and emotionally. These women supported me and encouraged me to pursue my dreams. The first woman's name is Traci. I met her at church.

When I met Traci, I was looking for a genuine friendship. Initially, we would hang out and pray together. As the friendship between Traci and I developed, she saw my heart and began to pour into me. We started going to financial classes together, and she gave me tips and techniques to help me get out of debt. With her help, I was able to pay down my debt and purchase my first home. She also encouraged me to pursue my dream of becoming an author. When I wrote my first book, she helped plan and organize my book signing. Traci taught me to be more polished in my demeanor so that I could attract the audience I wanted to reach.

During this genuine friendship, I gained a friend, a mentor, and a coach. Though she had never coached anyone before, Traci saw the potential that I saw in myself and knew that I would utilize the resources and assistance she poured into me. As a result of my transformation, Traci was inspired to start her own coaching and mentoring program while I pursued my dreams to become an author and a motivational speaker. So, the experience was mutually beneficial.

I met the second woman, Chloe, through her mother. Ironically, some of the same people that had something to say about the way I dressed or that I shouldn't have been struggling would say, "You shouldn't be Chole's friend because of who her mother is." Thankfully, I didn't pay that any mind. Chole has always been a great supporter and has encouraged me through some of my most difficult times. I can always rely on her to give me her honest opinion. Chole is very resourceful and has always given me insight on how to improve my projects and ideas. Despite what anyone else thought, she was a great friend to me.

After these experiences that have helped to shape me into the woman that I am today, I took it on as a responsibility to pay it forward and help other women who are searching in the way that I was.

Paying it Forward

As I pay it forward, here are several things that I would like to share to encourage and empower you both professionally and personally.

1. **Remember to Pursue Your Dreams**

   - Your dream is a gift, and it will make room for you.
   - Pursing your dreams will allow you a level of confidence in yourself that you never really knew you had.

2. **Don't Be Afraid to Make Mistakes**

   - Mistakes will happen, don't be afraid to fail.
   - Fear is a failure if it causes you not to try.

3. **You Won't Win Them All and That's Ok**

   - I look at a loss as a lesson.
   - A loss is an opportunity to improve and do something better the next time.

4. **Leave Negativity Behind**

   - Let go of negative thoughts and people.

- You won't be able to reach your highest potential holding onto negative energy.

5. Be Authentic

- You must be true to yourself.

- People may notice you from your outer appearance, but they will remember you by your character.

- Your character can open and close doors for you.

6. Be Coachable

- You must have a teachable spirit.

- Be willing to listen to the advice of those who are where you want to be and have been where you are.

- Be willing to do the work it takes to get you where you want to be.

7. Be Encouraged

- Surround yourself with other like-minded women who will support you and encourage you to pursue your dreams.

- If we as women would empower one another, we can achieve greatness.

Reflection

As you read these points of empowerment, what thoughts or emotions came up for you?

_____
_____
_____
_____
_____
_____
_____
_____
_____
_____
_____
_____
_____
_____

Farrah McBride

Farrah Daphane McBride is an author, poet and motivational speaker. As a child growing up in Augusta, Georgia, Farrah has always been creative. It was her dream to become an author. In 2016 that dream came true. She became the author of "*ABC's to Happiness* and *Diary 0723 Vol 1: Revealing Truth.*" Both books have inspired many to follow their dreams as well as to fight through some personal issues they may have experienced or may be experiencing. In 2017, Farrah landed a small part in a local stage play where she currently resides in Maryland. Today Farrah continues to be creative as she encourages and motivates others to pursue their dreams and realize that they are the key to unlocking their happiness.

Chapter Ten

No Place for Competition

In my opinion, the single most destructive thing that can happen to a friendship next to betrayal is competitiveness. There's no place for it in friendships. Listen, I am human, just like you. I know what it feels like to watch people get ahead of you in different areas of life, but I learned something that will change your life if you let it. Celebrate people even when they are doing better than you, even when they have the very thing that you want for yourself. This is how peace and joy will enter your life as relates to where you are. I also believe it's how you attract what you want to come into your life.

There is nothing joyous about being salty about someone else's accomplishments. You're still going to feel whatever emotions are there. It doesn't make you feel better. It does absolutely nothing for you except make you look like a hater. Be happy for your friends when they are happy. Celebrate their moments. I'm not talking about pretending to be happy to save face. If you can't genuinely be happy for your friends, you need to take a look inside of yourself. It should come naturally to find joy in those moments when the people that you love experience great things. The Bible tells us to, *"rejoice with them that do rejoice."* Romans 12:15 (KJV)

You and the people you have chosen as friends should be on the same team. A win for one should feel like a win for all. A true friend will want what is best for you, and most importantly, want for you what you want. In most cases, your friends can't wait to celebrate a win with you. They should not feel uncomfortable when it is their turn. They shouldn't feel like it's going to make you feel bad or unhappy because it didn't happen to you. That's not fair.

If you aren't living a life that you love, keep at it. Create the life that you crave and be okay when others get there first. Sometimes, the reason we haven't reached certain goals in life is because we are more focused on what other people are doing and accomplishing. Other times it's because we haven't done enough to achieve it. You can't be upset at someone else if you have not done the work. Instead, be vulnerable and ask your friend to help you get on track, to pray with you, or to show you how to reach the goal.

Comparing yourself to others is a dream killer, as I'm sure you've heard a million times before. The funny thing is that the people you secretly envy may also envy you. Our lives are not just quick snapshots. We have to look at the whole picture. My friends bought homes before me, had children before me, and got into committed relationships before me. However, I've done things before them too. I launched my business, got my credit to a perfect score, paid all my debt, and own most of my time. It's not a competition. I'm saying this to encourage you to look at your whole picture when you start to feel behind. Make sure that you only compare your accomplishments against your "to-do" list, not theirs. Beat your own best score and remember that the grass is not always greener in the other person's yard, and everything that glitters isn't gold.

You will get to where you want to be with consistency and by using your faith. It has nothing to do with the life that other people are living. We don't know God's plan for other people's lives. We can only hope that they do and that they are right where He wants them to be. Our job is to ensure that for ourselves. His plan for us is unique to us, and we must walk out our path one day at a time.

This Girl is Trippin'

What about when your friend is the one that seems to have the issue? I think at one time or another we have all encountered this friend. She is always speaking negatively to put a damper on your moments of excitement. She is quick to make a negative comment about your good news. She never really seems happy for you but will get upset when she is not celebrated. You know who I'm talking about.

I still laugh today when reflecting on a situation with a friend some years ago. She came to my house for the first time after having not seen me in a long while. Without being asked her opinion, she commented that she didn't like my neighborhood because guys were hanging out in the streets. I had been living there for five years and had never seen people just hanging out. I am very particular about where I live, and this would have been a concern of mine, had it been true. The truth is that I lived in a very nice neighborhood that I was happy with.

The same day she also mentioned how she didn't like my new car and would not have chosen that car for herself. I laughed and said something like, "Well, it's a good thing this isn't your car." It was a brand-new Acura, leather seats, sunroof, clean, and shiny. It was just what I wanted. I couldn't understand why she was sharing her opinion. I started to detect a little bit of the green-eyed monster.

The whole afternoon that we were together, she took every opportunity to share what she didn't like about me and my stuff right down to my hair and earrings. Inside I laughed because I knew what this was about. She was miserable and wanted me to be miserable too. She couldn't handle the fact that I was happy with my life. A few months after this almost unbearable exchange with her, she moved into the house across the street from mine in the neighborhood that she did not like. She liked it enough to purchase property there, apparently.

In every conversation we had, which I kept brief and far in between, whenever I spoke about any of the positive things I had going on, she either shot it down or said, "me too." She refused to let me just have something that was just about me and admit that it was nice or a good thing. If I spoke about something that was even a tad bit negative, she would blow it up really big. It was like it brought her joy to hear that something wasn't going right for me. I know I'm not the only one who has experienced this with a "friend."

I had to realize this was a problem within her. There was something about her that brought out a level of insecurity that didn't allow her to have positive relationships because she saw everyone as better than her. As a defense mechanism, she would try to bring other people down to her perceived level. Knowing this, I found it difficult to be upset with her. I also found it difficult to be her friend. Sometimes you just have to move on from people for your own sanity and let them figure out their own issues.

In life, we will meet all kinds of people who each come with their own set of issues. We all have them. Some of us learn how to overcome our issues and still form real bonds with others. However, this is not the case for everyone. Some people never reach that place. It's not completely their fault, but not taking any responsibility for it is why they remain where they are. We have to make the choice whether or not we are going to be in that place with them or move on from it.

All relationships are not permanent. You just must decide when it's time to walk away and when you're still in a phase where there is something to hold on to. There are even times when friendships fade out, and you pick them back up later after both people have grown, matured, and thought things through. So, every separation is not permanent. As we have all heard a million times, people come into our lives for a reason, a season, or a lifetime. If the reason has been resolved, it's okay to move on. If the season has passed, it's okay to move on. If the friendship is for a lifetime, nurture it.

Reflection

Have you ever dimmed your light to make a friend feel comfortable or to avoid making them feel bad or less accomplished? Why or why not?

_____
_____
_____
_____
_____
_____
_____
_____
_____
_____
_____
_____
_____

This next chapter, written by Megan, was so relatable for me as an entrepreneur who has experienced working with partners on projects and having slight issues there. I could also relate to just having friends in general who can tell you when you have dropped the ball, having those tough conversations that I described in the previous chapter. If you are in business or just a goal-focused woman, you will definitely understand this from both perspectives.

Meet Megan

Chapter Eleven

Snap Out of It!

I had just wrapped up my 3rd consecutive year of the *Dreams Do Come True Brunch*, and it was such a relief. After months of uncertainty due to a recent hurricane affecting a lot of Florida residents, we endured slow ticket sales, uncertainty with travel for talent, and delays in shipping the products we needed. However, we accomplished the goal of having a successful event, and our Keynote Speaker, Angela Yee delivered.

I was proud to have completed our 3rd installment, even though it was a struggle for me. Not just a challenge financially but mentally as well. I was a new mother who just endured marital growing pains and was still trying to find my footing with major life changes to adapt to. In my mind, I was doing the best I could to function and maintain a certain level of enthusiasm, meeting deadlines, and communicating with my business partner. Though the event met my expectations, deep down, I knew that I had not met my partner's nor those I held for myself.

A couple of weeks passed, and my business partner, Ci called to talk to me. I could tell by her tone that she was serious and really needed to get something off her chest. She and I had been partnering almost four years. We usually spoke every day and gave updates on what was going on in our lives. So, she knew there was a lot happening in mine. I had dropped the ball so many times while planning our last event that she had to pick up the slack.

I had always pulled my weight, put my all into projects, and took pride in my work ethic. This time was different and unusual for me. The conversation was indeed uncomfortable, but after she read me my rights and expressed herself, I fell quiet. Not from shame, but because I respected her and knew it was coming from a place of love. I knew that if I was to continue this relationship, I could not allow this to happen again. Before she ended our call, she left me with food for thought, "If this is something you want to do, you must be in a place where you are ready to grow."

I recall arguing with her, not in anger, but trying to make my point that I was trying my best with all I had going on. I was justifying everything that I had not done for the business. Yes, as partners, we argue. We are two smart and determined women who have opinions and different points of view, but most all, respect for one another. So, we keep it cute and know how to argue.

Planning events is a passion of mine. I desired to grow. Nonetheless, I was trying to find a comfortable space with my home life, and we all know that comfortability does not yield growth. The thought that something we had worked so hard to build could be halted because of lackadaisical actions was heartbreaking, especially because I didn't even see it as being lazy. I saw it as, "I have a lot going on, and I am doing what I can."

I thank God my sister in business didn't give up on me even though I had kind of given up on myself. I stopped getting my hair done, taking care of myself to my normal standards, and gained so much weight through the process. Ci's goal was to wake me up and let me know that I was slipping and needed to get it together. I remember her saying "What will happen is while you are taking your time, women who don't even have as much talent as you will surpass you, because they have the drive." That was the realest truth I had ever heard!

I had to start preparing myself for the next quarter, which required me to reflect and look in the mirror. I asked myself three pertinent questions:

1. Why did you start this business in the first place?

2. Is your work anywhere near complete?

3. Are you giving it your all?

After getting out of my feelings and hopping into my work, I went back and had another conversation with my sister Ci. Not Ci, the business partner, but Ci, my sister and friend, who even when she is disappointed in me, can lift me up and pour into me. Everyone deserves a sister like her in their corner. Someone who can be candid and straight forward, holding nothing back, but at the same time be understanding and compassionate.

We all have best friends we can talk to about certain things, but as an entrepreneur, we face different battles. I found myself upset with my best friends because they didn't support things I did. I don't have that issue now, because I understand that there are certain battles that only a person with the same drive and vision can understand. Your best friend who may be a teacher, will not give you the same advice as an entrepreneur friend when business gets stressful.

The teacher will tell you, "Slow down, take some time for yourself," which is not bad friend advice. The entrepreneur friend is going to think in terms of building a successful business and maybe offer some strategies to make things less stressful. The reason their advice is different is that their experiences and focus is different. I am not suggesting you get rid of your Day 1's, but you cannot expect them to relate to your struggle as an entrepreneur, their support is expressed starkly different.

In any relationship, whether it be business or personal, communication is key. Along with communication comes acknowledgment. If your partner presents a problem to you, if you want to continue the relationship, you change. Many people have issues with partnerships because there is always someone there to hold you accountable for your actions and pride takes over. Accountability is a factor that a lot of women need to accomplish a goal. However, accountability involves calling you out and demands you let go of bad habits. Accountability is needed because if we fall off our game, we make excuses for ourselves and fail to see where we went wrong. Having objective input is ideal.

A business partner is not necessary for everyone, but having a woman in business that you can call on when you find yourself overwhelmed is very important. She can be a sounding board, a "no" woman, or another woman to just laugh about a client you just hung up with. She can wear many hats depending on the day and what you are experiencing, but you need her. She is a part of your growth journey. She is your village and could end up being a collaborator on a dope project that you did not even have on your schedule until a late-night session with her.

Get To It!

Since my epiphany three years ago, when I vowed to never become that person who loses focus on their goals for comfortability, my partnership has been strong. I realized everything I had on my plate should propel me into my purpose and motivate me to stay the course. I had to find balance. This meant prioritizing my time to be a mother, wife, partner, and most of all, take time for myself. It was not easy, and the wild part about balance is that it constantly requires you to readjust.

Think about what it takes for you to physically readjust. First is a consciousness that something needs to change. You look around to assess what is out of place, turn, fidget, fix yourself then evaluate the success of the adjustment. Apply this to life shifts and changes and consider what is waiting for you after the work is complete. Now, imagine having someone behind you saying, "You're looking good sis! I see you!"

Finding my footing and hearing my business partner saying things like, "That's her! That's the Megan I love to see," was rewarding on its own, but seeing my life progress while making these much-needed changes was the greatest payoff. Now more than ever, anytime I get a chance to, I promote sisterhood and collaboration because it saved me from spiraling.

My biggest priority now is myself and my growth. Part of my growth was to expand my village of like-minded women. When you surround yourself with bosses, the conversations are different. It's one thing to talk about your next move, but to see other women executing and killing it, is a whole other level of motivation. I wanted to attract that too my life and offer that to someone else.

Though I created events for women to collaborate, I truly never stepped outside my circle until three years ago. I decided I wanted to go out more and do more when my husband and kids are at home. So, I started inviting women that I admired out for lunch and other events. I was surprised when they accepted. I discovered they also had similar struggles and even found it hard to find other women they trusted to be a part of their village. Now, do not go out there being too friendly and trusting everyone with your time and business. We should always be selective, trust our gut and not overshare, but do not be afraid to speak to a woman you think you could learn from.

My business partner and friend was not afraid to confront me and hold me accountable in a way that was beneficial to our partnership and our relationship as friends. I had to be able to receive what she was saying and do better. She could have held a grudge against me for dropping the ball or become passive aggressive towards me. I could have had an attitude that she spoke up about it. That would not have benefitted us at all, in fact, our relationship would have likely ended there.

Reciprocity is major in any relationship. You should give back what you receive. That includes encouragement and correction, in love. Not being able to do that is a sure-fire way to lose a part of your village. No one wants to feel used and pour so much into another person, to a point where they feel empty with nothing left for themselves. Some days, being in tune with those around you and actively listening takes precedence over what you have going on.

I have some questions for you:

When is the last time you ventured out and cultivated a new networking relationship?

After the follow on Instagram, Snap Chat, or Facebook, do you take the connection a step further?

Do you have anyone in your village that motivates you?

Was the last phone conversation that you had with a friend about money moves, credit, prospects, or anything to help you grow professionally?

If not, is there any contact in your phone with whom this would be the topic of conversation?

When is the last time you asked your sister in business if or how you could aid in her success?

When is the last time you collaborated with another woman on a project?

     If you have no problem answering these questions, I am proud of you, and I guarantee that you are on the right track. Your village is strong, and you are a pillar in it. If you had to think too hard or had no idea about any of these questions, then there is work to be done. Get to it!

     I hope that my story has helped you in some way and wish you much success on your journey to being the boss I know you can be. Be open for advice from the individuals that have your best interest at heart and want to see you be better than you are today. I promise you that some of your biggest cheerleaders and accountability partners are women that you have not even broken the ice with yet. Do not allow fear of rejection to hinder you from growing your network and let go of the fallacy that women cannot work together. I have discovered that the greatest movements involved multiple players! A woman who shares your experiences, is your greatest ally.

Reflection

Megan described being confronted with the fact that she dropped the ball and needed to get it together. Can you receive this type of criticism from people in your life who care?

Do you give this type of criticism, or do you shy away from any form of confrontation or uncomfortable conversations? Why?

Megan Johnson

Megan Johnson is a mother, wife and entrepreneur. A graduate from the University of South Florida, where she gained her degree in Health Science, her passion for environmental health led her to a career in energy. During her tenure, people noticed Megan's eye for coordinating events and decor. What started off as a hobby, she decided to turn into a business (Ci Me In Your Dreams Enterprises) Where she consults and helps others create, brand and market their events. Her latest venture is her Design business, where she uses her decorating experience to transform spaces and branding experience to transform business aesthetics.

In this last chapter Ilka shares her experiences with bullying even as an adult and then how she overcame those trials and went on the become one of the biggest supporters of women. She shares her best tips for being confident and bold and loving yourself for who you are. This is so important for women of all ages, but especially our young women who face so many challenges trying to meet the expectations of the media and their peers.

Meet Ilka

Chapter Twelve

From Crushed to Confident

When I was a little girl, I had a tendency to like anything related to arts. I remembered saying to my mom that I wanted to be a ballerina. It was not that weird in the sense that my mom and my grandma used to sing at church, and my dad used to do drama also, so it's in my veins. I was a very extroverted girl. I used to sing and participate in dramas at church. I wasn't afraid to perform in front of people. It was in my nature. I loved taking photos and being the center of attention. I was in every family pictures by default.

Middle school is when everything about how I felt about myself changed. I started to deal with bullying. I started to feel uncomfortable around others and totally insecure about who I was. By that time, I wore eyeglasses, was very thin and nerdy. I was the perfect target for kids with insecurities. In most cases bullying reflects a person's lack of self-confidence. At that time, didn't understand that. It took me years to understand the concept of confidence as the foundation of self-love. My relationships with girls around me by that point weren't positive. I didn't trust them because they were bullying me, and it made me feel bad.

As a result of the intense bullying that I suffered, I was feeling ugly and insecure. I stopped doing what I loved to do, performing arts. I was no longer motivated to perform and felt very vulnerable around people who would make me feel bad about my appearance. I was no longer an extroverted young girl. I changed into an insecure and vulnerable teenager.

They said that being a teenager is tough. My adolescence was the worst. Normally adolescents are extremely concerned about how they look. What others think about you, and sexual attractiveness start at this phase too. Imagine that, plus people telling you that you are ugly, you will never get a boyfriend, that you looked like Olive Oyl from Popeye. I was made fun of for being a nerd and was told that my glasses made me look worse. It was devastating and my confidence was destroyed by classmates who didn't even realize the effect that their words had.

Confidence was an important issue for me, but at a certain point, it became my strongest feature. Why is confidence so important? Self-confidence is believing and feeling comfortable in yourself and your own skin and knowing your worth. Being the extrovert and pulling on the self-esteem I had before, I decided not to let people crush my self-image.

One day I was at a mall, and a girl from a booth pulled me away and told me: You should be a model. I said to myself, "You're crazy. I don't even want people to look at me, and you are telling me I should model?" Well, I never imagined that this modeling "thing" would change my whole life. I went home excited, but we didn't have the money to pay for a modeling course. I decided to drop the whole idea and excitement of becoming a model. I decided modeling was for rich and beautiful people, not me. One day I received a call from the modeling school. They expressed interest in me and offered me a scholarship to attend!

By that time, my feelings of insecurity started to change. I was excited about the possibility of becoming a model and decided to challenge myself and start classes. I wanted to find my spark again. I knew that being confident and assertive would open doors for me that were once closed by the experience of being bullied. Developing this in myself was not optional. It was mandatory and could be applied to every area of my life. I was ready for this journey!

Confidence attracts people to you and makes them pay attention. When you feel good about yourself, it shows and commands the room! It can get you hired for better jobs, attracts better clients, and creates opportunities. I've been accused of displaying a sense of arrogance in interviews, but it's gotten me the kind of jobs I dreamed about.

Self-confidence can also scare people who aren't confident in themselves, because it is an unspoken challenge for them to grow in an area they may not be ready to face. On the other hand, it helps you aim for your dreams and desires. If you don't believe in yourself, no one will.

If you want to live well and achieve your dreams, you need to be sure of your own abilities. If not, opportunities will be presented to you, but you will not feel worthy of them. When you have high self-esteem, you choose yourself over others without trying to please people. You make decisions based on your core values and desires, and stand confidently, knowing what you're choosing is right for you. Self-confidence helps you to be productive. You will spend your time on activities, people, and tasks that will help you achieve your goals.

Understanding the benefits of having high self-esteem, I made the decision to improve myself in the areas I was struggling in, including relationships and bonds with other women. My modeling classes were a game-changer. They taught me to believe in what I could achieve, be disciplined, perfect my techniques in runway and photography, as well as how to take care of my skin, hair, makeup, etc. I started to create good relationships with the other girls and the instructor in the classroom. I started to trust women in general. When I was bullied, it was predominately from women, so my trust in them as support was nonexistent. The classes helped me break down those walls of distrust.

With every class, I made my transformation to become who I am today. I am a totally self-assured woman who teach others how to be confident in themselves and create positive relationships. Confidence is my main weapon of success in life. Why? If I believe in myself, I will make you believe in me, and consequently, my message of believing in self will materialize through my story. Everything I achieved as a model and person had to be related to my own self-image.

My first modeling school back in my hometown of Puerto Rico was called Metamorphosis. I chose to use the same name for my mentorship program because it means to a change the form or nature of a thing or person into a completely different version, by natural or supernatural means. My program focuses on the transformation of women who desire to develop self-confidence and to nurture friendships with other women.

I always tell my students that a good tribe of women is hard to defeat. Each woman defends and supports her fellow members by making strong bonds of affection and respect that thrive through adversity. Let me clarify that even in the modeling industry, there is bullying. The bullying didn't stop because I became a model; it got worse, but I was better equipped to deal with it. I stayed focused on what I needed to learn and to be prepared to start my modeling career successfully.

What do you picture when you think of a model's lifestyle? I know the first thing that comes to our minds is glamour, beauty, and luxury, but let me tell you there's more than what meets the eye. To make it in the industry, you have to fight hardship and negativity. So, on my first casting call, I was excited. It was my big opportunity to showcase my talent. However, one of the casting directors' feedback was that I was ugly and looked too exotic. I wasn't tall enough, and I would never be a model. He never criticized my runway modeling or casting picture. He just focused on how he could bring me down about my appearance.

His words didn't affect me at all. I said thanks and left. My modeling instructor prepared me for that. Afterwards, I had so many casting calls that I lost track of them. Bullying in modeling can either come from less successful models, people who don't understand the industry, or people within the industry that don't want you to succeed. So, don't think that as a model bullying is not something I still deal with. The difference is I know how to deal with it, and I teach my modeling students how to kill people with kindness.

The model of confidence: secure, confident, and empowered

It is not easy talking about myself being an insecure person in the past, but by sharing my experience, I may be able to help others who may be struggling in the same areas. There isn't one person among us who doesn't have some insecurity. Some are just good at hiding them. We worry too much about what people think about us and how we look to others, about failing, or that in the end, people will think we're a fraud. We pay too much attention to social media opinions regarding who we're supposed to be. We spend too much time looking for attention, likes and shares. I'm not saying it is not a part of our daily lifestyle, but we need to stop allowing the opinions of others to determine who we are and what we can achieve.

How do I overcome the insecurities? I face what is uncomfortable to face and take action to change it. There were some obstacles that I had to overcome when I started my modeling classes. Remember, I was totally insecure so getting exposure was a big deal for me. I had to face past criticism by others, a negative self-image, needing the approval of others, lack of trust in myself, and not accepting my flaws as a woman.

We all have flaws. No one is perfect. When you see a celebrity, model, singer, etc. they have been produced by a team of people around them like stylists, designers, hair and makeup, aesthetics, publicist, and other professionals who work to create their image. That means whatever you think looks perfect on a photo, a video, or a magazine is not as perfect as it seems.

To overcome my insecurities, I started to practice these exercises, and even to this day, if I get caught on those thoughts, I put them in practice and it has helped me to accept and embrace who I am and where I want to go in life, accepting everything that comes with being me.

- I forget my past and all the people that bullied me.
- I accept myself, the good, the bad, and the ugly.
- I always look for ways to improve myself without taking away from my uniqueness.
- I trust my ability to make sound decisions based on my experiences and instincts.

When I started my first modeling class, I was the shyest student in the group. One of the first classes we took was self-confidence. That class made me realize everything I felt after bullying could be changed if I believed in myself. The photo-posing class was one of my best classes ever. I learned how to pose in front of the camera, how to recognize my best angles, and how to express different emotions. During this class, all my doubts and insecurities started to crumble down. When we got to runway class, it was a real struggle for me. I had to walk in front of people and be judged? No way that was going to happen!

My modeling instructor was an important piece of this puzzle. She believed in me and my capacity to overcome my fears. I learned the correct techniques, timing, and posing on the runway, so I wasn't afraid anymore. I went to class every Saturday and practiced at home between every class. I implemented the quote, "practice makes perfect." I wasn't perfect but I kept practicing and successfully modeling on the runway was a huge step in the right direction.

I also took public speaking class, something that I still use today. All those tools helped me get out of my shell and become stronger both personally and professionally. It was not comfortable for me to trust myself, but I took the risk and succeeded.

I was offered a position as a modeling intern. Next, I started as a modeling instructor. I also participated in two beauty pageants. 20 years after my first pageant, I decided to challenge myself again by representing Puerto Rico as Mrs. Puerto Rico Millennium Universe 2020. I never stopped challenging myself. It is a part of the process of growing as an individual and professional.

Professional development is key, and I took several certifications as a model, modeling instructor, actor, etc. If you want to be taken seriously in your industry, you must take risks, be prepared, and make a name for yourself. To increase my exposure and reach more women, I started a fashion, beauty, and confidence blog, where I share my tips and tricks.

My career as a model has opened a lot of doors, not only in modeling but in other industries as well. I decided to stay in the arts because it has been my passion for as long as I can remember, but I have a bachelor's degree in biology/ pre-medic and 12 years in the medical industry. Why did I mention this? I mentioned it because it is about what fills your heart. Even though I studied and love what I learned while pursuing my degree, I didn't feel passionate about it.

Many people see modeling as a superficial, fake industry. I see it as my opportunity to share the same tools that helped me overcome my insecurities with girls, teens, and other women. Being confident comes from within. Through my experience, others in the same situation can acquire what took me a long time and a lot of effort to learn. Every time I teach my modeling classes, I grow stronger and convinced of my purpose, which is being their mentor. I teach them how to grow into the best version of themselves, become stronger, determined, and resilient so life situations won't pull them down. I make sure they know, if I overcame it, they can too.

I'm a mentor, guide, empowered woman, and visionary. I want my students to achieve the same or even higher goals than me. When you become a mentor or an instructor, your end goal is making your students a better version of themselves. Supporting women creates bonds of trust and equality. I look to create relationships with my students that goes far beyond just being their mentor. I want them to see me as a friend in which I support them, and they support me.

Some people asked me: Why do you teach them all that you know and had to struggle for 20 years to achieve? The answer is simple, when you have talents and abilities, it is our job to help others with them. As the cliché says, "with great power, there must also come great responsibility." Truer words have never been spoken. When you feel passionate about something, you want to spread your passion so others can feel the same passion for what you do.

My students are my legacy. My relationship with them is more than just an instructor. I am a mentor who wants to see them succeed. If they succeed, I succeed. My purpose and vision are fulfilled through them. The way to achieve your purpose in life is to help yourself so that you can help others. That is the best gift that I can give to someone else.

Reflection

Have you ever felt less than confident? What changed that for you, or do you still struggle with this?

_____
_____
_____
_____
_____
_____
_____
_____

What advice would you give a young woman who struggles with confidence?

_____
_____
_____
_____
_____
_____
_____
_____
_____
_____

Ilka Tamar

Ilka is an entrepreneur, professional model, certified modeling and confidence instructor, blogger, and influencer. She is recognized for instructing modeling as a tool of self-confidence and empower-ment, allowing girls, youth and adults to learn through their modeling workshops and fashion blog equally with the foundations and techniques on how to be models and enhance their image as a brand. She has more than 20 years of experience as a model, participating in countless catwalks, events, editorials, and pageants competitions in Puerto Rico and the United States among others. Her passion is to teach modeling as an enriching tool of self-confidence to each student, making them achieve a remarkable inside-out metamorphosis. Leaving a legacy with her work is her mission for future generations.

She's the CEO and founder of:

- Modish Bold Squad- Fashion, Beauty and confidence Blog
- Metamorphosis Mentorship-Online Modeling and Confidence Program
- Miss/Mrs Puerto Rico Millennium Universe-National Beauty Pageant Franchise Owner

www.ilka-tamar.com

Her motto is: Confidence is everything!

To My Girls

We asked some friends on social media some questions about friendship, and this is what they had to say...

Shannon Wilkerson
Yesterday at 4:45pm

What are your friendship expectations?

👍❤️ 100   49 Comments 7 Shares

👍 Like   ➤ Share

View more 16 Comments

Trisha Fowler I expect my friends to support me in my endeavors. Not necessarily financially, but spiritually, emotionally, and socially.
❤️ 10
Like · Reply · 1h

Angela Parker I expect a return on the investments that I make in my friendships. I want to feel fortified and enriched, not depleted.
❤️ 8
Love · Reply · 1h

Shatika Wages Loyalty and respect are my two major expectations. With both of those qualities in place, we can get through anything, build success, and have plenty of breakthroughs
❤️ 12
Love · Reply · 1h

Tina Silas My friendship expectation is to be respected even in our differences as we grow, mature, and change.
❤️ 6
Like · Reply · 2h

Paula Milner I expect a judgment free zone and no competition. I also expect my friends to be truthful and supportive.

Like · Reply · 2h ⚪⚪ 3

 Debbie Stokes I expect a friend to be there not only for the good times, but during the dark times as well. Too often people leave your side when you are in real trouble, hurting, sick, etc.

Love · Reply · 2h ⚪⚪ 9

 Mayra Figueroa-Clark I expect my friends to be comfortable challenging my thoughts so that we may have productive conversations about religion, racism, or love.

Love · Reply · 2h ⚪⚪ 15

 DL Hutchinson Tell me the truth even if you think it will hurt me. I'd rather hear it from a friend.

Love · Reply · 3h ⚪⚪ 20

 Tiffany Dillard I expect my friends to be an emotionally safe place for me. Having a friend who is always negative will cause me to pull back.

Like · Reply · 3h ⚪⚪ 3

 Danielle Pope Love me enough to check me. I don't want "yes" friends.

Love · Reply · 4h ⚪⚪ 18

 Rielle LaNoir Love I expect loyalty and all that it encompasses. I want my friends to tell me when I'm wrong. However, if I don't listen, I don't want my friends to say, "I told you so." I already know that.

Like · Reply · 4h ⚪⚪ 5

 Write a comment...

Friendship Prayer

Lord, I thank you for the women that you have placed in my life whom I call friend. I am so grateful that you have connected us and have been at the center of our friendships. You help us to approach our friendship from a place of love, understanding and support and guide us in the best ways to do so. Thank you, God, for removing people from my life who did not have my best interest or your heart towards me. Continue to help me to be the best possible me and to provide the level of friendship that you want for all of us.

It is in the name of Jesus that I pray,

Amen

Add Your Friendship Story

To My Girls

www.ingramcontent.com/pod-product-compliance
Lightning Source LLC
Chambersburg PA
CBHW071114030426
42336CB00013BA/2077